THE TYRANNY OF

TWO PERCENT

Geoffrey C. Jackson

Jackson Consulting Group, LLC

Litchfield Park, AZ

Jackson
Consulting
Group, LLC

ISBN-13: 979-8-9953899-0-3 (paperback)
ISBN-13: 979-8-9953899-1-0 (digital)

Printed in the United States of America

TABLE OF CONTENTS

INTRODUCTION

To the manufacturing leaders who have spent years meticulously perfecting their operations but are struggling with continuously delivering on those year over year savings—this book is for you.

You've implemented Lean Manufacturing, mastered Six Sigma, and championed countless continuous improvement initiatives. You've successfully wrung out significant waste and inefficiency from your production lines, supply chains, and administrative processes. Yet, you've likely reached a familiar inflection point: the traditional toolkit, while powerful, is yielding diminishing returns. Squeezing out the next round of transformative savings or efficiency gains through purely analog methods feels increasingly like trying to push a rope. A wall has been hit. You've heard about the Industry 4.0 revolution but the software systems you have today aren't making the difference you had hoped they would.

The solution is not more of the same, but a change in how you approach digitization. You have already heard that this journey promises the next step-change in productivity, resilience, and competitive

* * *

advantage, connecting your entire operational ecosystem—from the shop floor sensors to the executive dashboard—in real-time.

However, the path is fraught with complexity. Digital transformation is not merely an IT/OT project; it is a profound organizational change. It requires new mindsets, new governance models, and, most importantly, a clear understanding of the common pitfalls. This book addresses the real challenges facing production improvements in a mature environment. It offers a practical guide for how to approach your journey and avoid the pitfalls that take down most digital transformation efforts.

I have been in the trenches of multiple digital transformation efforts across various manufacturing industries and levels of digital maturity. I have personally been involved in the projects that stalled, the technologies that were prematurely adopted, and the cultural clashes that undermined brilliant strategies. Put simply, I've made a lot of the mistakes this book seeks to help you avoid. But I have also learned the lessons and seen first-hand how to achieve successful deployment and achieve real savings.

My goal in writing this is to synthesize those hard-won learnings into practical guidance, a roadmap for success that is grounded in the realities of manufacturing operations, not just theoretical blueprints. This book is intended to provide the clarity, structure, and cautionary tales necessary to ensure your digital transformation journey delivers on its promise. Let's break through the wall together.

"A must read for the Operations executive" - Peter Antonucci COO Ashton Informatics

"A relatable and refreshingly honest look at digital transformation in manufacturing- surfacing the quiet pitfalls, organizational blind spots, and execution realities." - Lauren Harrington Regional Director Services and Solutions Rockwell Automation

CHAPTER 1: THE BUDGET CHALLENGE

Mark Donaldson, VP of Operations for Omnicron Products, ran a hand across his scalp, feeling the familiar prickle of a late-stage workday headache. The clean, crisp white noise from the high-efficiency HVAC unit was the only sound in the second-floor corner office. Outside the expansive, double-paned window, the meticulously landscaped corporate park shimmered under the afternoon sun, a serene contrast to the anxiety tightening in his chest.

He swiveled slightly in his chair, the precision bearings silent. On the sleek, pale wood desk, the quarterly operations report burned on the left monitor, its illuminated dashboard a cold, undeniable alarm. The critical metrics, stark red against a muted gray background, were a punch to the gut—a sight he scanned with mounting desperation and a frustrated sigh.

Metric	Previous year	Projection
Total Revenue	$310M	$310M
Cost of Goods Sold	$252.4M	$248M
Gross Margin	$57.6M	$62M
Gross Margin Percentage	18.5%	20.00%

A tight, burning knot formed in his stomach. *Twenty percent.*

The annual margin goal, etched in stone by the executive board and relentlessly championed by CFO Brian Quince, was twenty-two percent. Two percentage points. A seemingly insignificant decimal, yet it represented 6.2 million dollars in phantom cost savings that he simply could not find.

For eight years, Mark and his team had been miracle workers. They'd squeezed between two and four percent in cost reduction every single year. They'd optimized logistics, hammered down supplier prices, rationalized product lines, and wrung every drop of efficiency from their aging, sprawling manufacturing base. He'd celebrated the victories, but now, staring at the diminishing returns, he felt less like an optimizer and more like a desperate gambler playing a rigged game. He shut down the computer, the sudden darkness in the room mirroring the intellectual darkness of his predicament. He just didn't know where the next cut was going to come from. There was no fat left. They were slicing bone.

● ● ●

The presentation the next morning was a polished, professional ritual of pain. Mark delivered the numbers with his usual calm, authoritative demeanor, detailing the projected market growth and the mitigation of raw material costs. He concluded with the margin, the twenty percent.

Brian Quince, a man whose tailored suits always looked slightly sharper than everyone else's, didn't even raise an eyebrow. He simply steepled his fingers, his eyes, cold as glacial ice, fixed on Mark.

"Mark," Brian's voice was smooth, devoid of inflection. "Excellent work on sustaining performance in a tightening market. Truly. Now, about that twenty-two percent. Where is it?"

Mark cleared his throat. "Brian, we've reached a point of diminishing returns on traditional cost-saving measures. To find the remaining two percent—the 6.2 million—without impacting our capacity or product quality, frankly, I don't see a clear path."

A collective sigh of corporate disappointment seemed to fill the room.

● ● ●

Brian's expression remained unchanged, a perfect mask of reasonable expectation. "Mark, you have a week. Find the clear path. I need a fully reconciled budget, meeting all stated goals, in my inbox next Friday morning. Until then, the twenty percent is... unacceptable."

Mark nodded, his jaw tight. He had a week to conjure 6.2 million dollars out of thin air. The mood in the room had shifted from exhaustion to desperation; the old ways of finding efficiency were spent, and an impossible expectation hung heavy over the Operations team.

● ● ●

CHAPTER 2: THE SPARK OF REVELATION

The following Monday morning, Mark was still battling the budget, a dense fog of frustration enveloping him. His desk was littered with printouts, P&L statements, CapEx reports, and a crumpled page where he'd tried to doodle a new, miraculously cheap manufacturing process. The demand for 6.2 million dollars felt like a waking nightmare.

When his assistant, Sarah, buzzed him about a meeting he'd agreed to the week prior, he almost cancelled. "It's Eric Washington, the Phoenix Engineering Manager, and Brett Miller, the Plant Manager. That thirty-minute software demo you agreed to as a distraction?" she reminded him gently. Mark sighed, running a hand through his perpetually neat silver hair. "Send them in. Thirty minutes, Sarah. No more."

Eric Washington, sharp and earnest, carried a sleek tablet and a quiet confidence. Brett Miller, the Plant

Manager, was older, built like a brick wall, and looked perpetually skeptical.

"Thanks for your time, Mr. Donaldson," Eric began, projecting a screen onto the wall. "We wanted to show you what we've been piloting in Phoenix for the past six months."

"Make it quick, Eric. Another Manufacturing Execution System? Another dashboard?"

"Respectfully, sir, no," Eric said, undeterred. "It's a data capture and analysis tool specifically focused on operational friction. We call the project 'Phoenix Rising,' at the plant."

The screen shifted, displaying a dense graph. It wasn't the usual Overall Equipment Effectiveness (OEE) metric Mark was accustomed to. It was a visualization of machine downtime events for a single product line: the high-volume 'Alpha-9' connector.

"The problem with traditional OEE," Eric explained, "is that it averages out the *why*. We knew the Alpha-9

● ● ●

line had a consistent, maddening four-hour downtime every other day. Our traditional tracking just listed it as 'Maintenance.' This tool goes deeper."

He zoomed in on a cluster of red dots on the timeline. "We integrated sensors on the feed mechanisms and used this software to auto-tag the exact moment of failure. It turns out, that four-hour block wasn't one big job. It was thirty separate micro-stoppages, each lasting between five and twenty minutes."

Brett finally spoke up, a note of grudging respect in his gravelly voice. "We always thought it was the material feed getting jammed up. Common sense, right? But the software showed us it was a specific interaction between the hydraulic pressure drop and the vibration from the cooling unit when it cycled on. A common cause variation we'd been dealing with for years, baked right into our process."

"What did you do?" Mark asked, leaning forward, the budget forgotten for the first time all week.

"Simple mechanical fix, cost us $5,000 for a stabilizing bracket and a minor code adjustment on the cooling unit. But the result..." Eric navigated to a different chart.

Metric	Baseline (Months 1-6)	Post-Implementation (Months 7-12)	Percentage Improvement
Alpha-9 Throughput	15,000 units/day	18,600 units/day	24.0%

"We integrated sensors on the feed mechanisms and used this software to auto-tag the exact moment of failure. It turns out, that four-hour block wasn't one big job. It was thirty separate micro-stoppages, each lasting between five and twenty minutes."

Mark stared at the 24.0%. A single item. Six months of data. A seemingly simple software tool targeting **common cause variation**, an issue that often fell into the blind spot between engineering and maintenance.

Mark stood up, dismissing the headache and the lingering exhaustion. The feeling was electric, a sudden, blinding flash of clarity. It wasn't about squeezing two percent out of logistics anymore. It was about unlocking a hidden, systemic, twenty-four percent waiting to be found in the noise of their operations.

"Gentlemen," Mark said, the weariness gone from his voice, replaced by a sudden, intense focus. "You may have just shown me where 6.2 million dollars is hiding." The tyranny of two percent had suddenly been challenged by the potential of twenty-four percent, proving that the solution wasn't to cut deeper, but to see smarter. Mark realized their future wasn't in cost reduction, but in digital insight.

CHAPTER 3: THE REVELATION AT HOME

The week concluded with Mark submitting the budget. On paper, it met the CFO's 22% margin goal. He'd penciled in 'Systemic Operational Efficiency Improvement' and assigned it a nebulous, required cost reduction. A 6.2-million-dollar bluff based only on a flash of conviction from a Phoenix engineer. He knew he was gambling, and the anxiety was a knot in his chest. He needed a framework, a philosophy. Something real to justify the number.

As Spring was approaching, he tried to put the office out of his mind, but the pressure was a constant hum. One weekend in late March, he walked out to his yard, determined to tackle a patch of lawn where aggressive dandelions and crabgrass had become an annual nemesis. This was always his therapy, a simple, tangible problem he could physically fix.

He started on his knees with a small hand trowel, digging at the roots. Sweat beaded on his forehead under the late afternoon sun. *Just pull them out, Mark. It's not rocket science,* he muttered to himself. But the roots kept snapping. He'd pull ten, and two days later, twenty more would appear, stronger, deeper. He had used expensive, non-targeted weed killers before, only to see the chemicals weaken the grass while the toughest weeds survived, their roots untouched.

Symptom, not root cause, a voice echoed in his mind— the ghost of Eric Washington's logic. *We're treating the symptom (the visible leaves) with an expensive, generic fix, just like we throw temporary labor at a machine breakdown.*

He sat back on his heels, the trowel hot in his hand. The truth hit him: he wasn't managing a problem; he was managing a symptom. The real issue was the poor soil, the inconsistent moisture retention, the fundamental *ecosystem* that favored the weeds over the grass. He needed data: soil pH, nutrient levels, and a water cycle analysis. He needed to stop reacting to the weeds and start managing the entire system proactively.

About a week later, sitting in the dark kitchen with a cup of tea, he stared at the new smart thermostat he'd installed last month. The old dial was simple: set the temp, and the AC ran until it hit the mark. The new one was different. It was integrated with his phone and local weather data. It didn't wait for the house to get cold or hot; it learned. It knew his commute, knew when a cold blast or a heat wave was forecast, and started heating or cooling the house proactively ten minutes before he arrived.

It wasn't just automating a manual task, he realized, the revelation hitting him like a jolt of electricity. It was using external data and personalized patterns to achieve an outcome—comfort at the lowest possible energy cost.

The next morning in his office, he stood up and walked to the window. He was still thinking about the weed pulling and thermostat and how that applied to the current state of affairs. His house was a microcosm of Omnicron Products, but exactly how was still a mystery. Phoenix had shown him that digital tools were absolutely the right solution, but which tools for which problems? He knew there was something there but he couldn't quite put his finger on it.

• • •

CHAPTER 4: DIGITAL OVERLOAD

M ark spent the next two days immersed in the annual **Global Industrial Optimization Conference**, wandering the vast convention hall with the focused intensity of a man looking for a life raft. The hall was a dizzying kaleidoscope of flashing LED screens and aggressive sales pitches. Every vendor promised the same thing: instant, transformative success.

The booths were a testament to the digital noise he was trying to navigate. *Opti-Max 3000: 30% OEE Gain in 90 Days!* screamed one banner. Another booth, sleek and minimalist, touted *The Process Whisperer: AI-Driven Cost Reduction* with a guaranteed two-month ROI. He collected a dozen glossy brochures, all promising quick implementation, reduced labor costs, and an increase in profitability that would make Brian Quince weep with joy. The sheer volume of choice was overwhelming, a digital supermarket of solutions where everything claimed to be the final answer.

Despite the chaos, Mark felt a fundamental conviction solidify: software was the key. Traditional methods had reached their limit. The only way to find the hidden 6.2 million dollars, the only way to beat the tyranny of two percent, was to invest heavily in the tools that could see the invisible friction on his factory floors. He felt a potent blend of hope and panic—hope that the solution was truly out there, and panic that he had no idea which glittering box to open first. He needed a strategic partner, not just a vendor, but in the frenzy of the conference, all he found were vendors shouting over each other.

Despite the chaotic nature of the conference, Mark's mind kept returning to the four distinct operational fiefdoms under his command, each representing a unique cultural hurdle to any unified digital strategy. Phoenix, under Brett Miller, embodied the *Show Me* culture; they were willing to try new things, but only if the solution was demonstrably earned and validated by their own engineers, as the Alpha-9 success proved. Dallas, led by the eager Gene Johnson, was the *Compliance* plant; they would enthusiastically execute any mandate Mark handed down, trusting corporate direction perhaps too readily. Pittsburgh, managing a specialized, high-mix product set, was the *Capacity* challenge; Rebecca's team was so stretched simply keeping production running that any new initiative, no matter how simple, felt like an impossible demand on their limited resources. And finally, there was Chicago with Vinny DiCarlo—the *Resistance* culture—a powerhouse of profitability that proudly operated on gut instinct and spreadsheets, often delivering results but fundamentally refusing to adopt any process they hadn't invented themselves.

That weekend, the struggle wasn't at his desk, but in the yard with a mountain of grass that needed to be cut. He walked into the garage, intending to perform basic maintenance on his ancient riding lawnmower. He fumbled with the dipstick, shining his phone light into the poorly lit engine bay, trying to match the oil level to the faded illustration in the thick, poorly organized manual. *A perfect analog for Omnicron's SOP binders,* he thought. *Confusing, generic, and designed for compliance, not clarity.*

He heard a soft clinking sound and turned to see his wife Emily watching him from the doorway, leaning against the frame, the tablet still in her hand from entering her student's grades.

"Still battling the weeds, or are you fighting with the mower now?" she asked, a gentle amusement in her tone.

"Both," he admitted, wiping grease on his jeans. "I'm trying to figure out if it needs an oil change, but the manual just says 'every 50 hours of operation,' and I haven't tracked that since 2018. It's reactive maintenance based on a generic schedule." He gestured toward his neighbor's newer, humming machine. "That thing has a little LED panel that probably just says: Oil Life: 85%. It knows what it needs and when it needs it. It has its own digital identity."

Emily walked over, putting a hand on his shoulder. "So your dipstick and a faded manual are like those work systems you are always telling me about? It's telling you to fix the machine only *after* it has already run a generic amount of time. What was that stuff that your Phoenix plant was talking about? Getting the right information at the right time?"

Mark looked at his wife, his eyes widening with recognition. "Yes! We're not looking at real-time condition—engine cycles, temperature spikes, wear data. We're relying on a calendar and a guess. The solution isn't a better manual; it's a predictive, data-aware machine." Maybe this was the place that we needed to start. The digital solution is a chaotic, unproven hypothesis, but the potential of the Alpha-9's 24% gain offered a blinding flash of hope that the path to transformation was real.

Mark went to his desk, the Spring flowers beginning to bloom behind him in the window, grabbed his laptop, and started drafting an email to the plant managers. The weariness was gone, replaced by a sudden, intense focus. He titled the draft: The Digital Transformation Initiative. Although the details of the plan were still as murky as the Chicago River after the St. Patrick's Day dyeing, a shift was about to occur.

The essence of the slides were:

The Mistake: The Tyranny of Two Percent	The Lesson: The Revelation at Home
Focusing on the Wrong Problem: Our traditional focus was only on finding cost reductions to meet the 22% margin goal, which had been achieved through "slicing bone" for eight years. This was an unsustainable, reactive approach.	The Shift to Finding Value: The 24% throughput gain in Phoenix proved the value was hidden in systemic *operational friction* (common cause variation), not in logistics or labor cuts.
Fixing the Symptom: Mark realized his operations were like his weed-infested lawn or his manual-based lawnmower—they were only ever fixing the *symptom* (the visible weed, the broken part) after the problem occurred.	The Proactive Mindset (Industry 4.0): Transformation means managing the *ecosystem* (soil, process, water) to prevent the problem in the first place, using real-time data to move from reactive to predictive action.
The Blind Bluff: Mark submitted the budget with a $6.2M "Systemic Operational Efficiency Improvement" line item, but he lacked the actual plan or framework to execute it.	Vision Must Precede the Plan: The domestic revelations provided the philosophical framework needed to justify the number. The Digital Transformation Initiative is not a list of tools but a fundamental shift in perception and management.

CHAPTER 5: THE PITFALLS OF ENTHUSIASM

Mark walked out of the mid-year executive summit feeling less like an operations guru and more like a visionary. The CEO, David McAllister, had just wrapped up a presentation on the need for a 22% corporate margin - a massive jump from the current 18.5% which is less than even the 20% Mark thought he would get. The mandate was clear: innovate, optimize, or face the wrath of Brian.

He gathered his four Plant Managers, Gene, Brett, Rebecca, and Vinny, less like a leader giving direction and more like a feverish general handing out weapons he hadn't tested. He mistook his own panic for decisive leadership. "The numbers *must* move, and move *now*!" he declared, his voice buzzing with the energy of a thousand new ideas. "Go find that hidden opportunity. No corporate approval needed. Just get it done!"

"We've seen the future and it's available *today*! Explore that digital landscape, bring back and deploy the best tools to optimize your plant. Find those savings and make them a reality. Just get it done and show me the results!"

The immediate results were a catastrophe of good intentions. At the Q2 review meeting in July, the plants reported out on the initial progress.

- **Dallas (Gene Johnson):** Gene, ever the eager early adopter, went for the flashiest option: **Prognosys**, a massive predictive maintenance and scheduling suite. Mark remembered Gene's email, full of exclamation points and buzzwords. Gene saw it as a gold medal for Dallas, promising a 5% margin boost. Mark felt a surge of pride—*at least one of them got it.*

- **Phoenix (Brett Miller):** Brett, the pragmatic veteran, was wary of flash. He opted for **MetricMonk**, an OEE tracker known for its flexibility and made by the same supplier of the tool that got him the 24% improvement earlier. "If we can't measure it, we can't manage it," Brett had stated plainly, not realizing that "flexibility" meant they could redefine "downtime" to exclude half the working week, artificially inflating their OEE to an impossible 98%.

- **Pittsburgh (Rebecca Stevens):** Mark's heart ached for Rebecca in Pittsburgh, the smaller, higher-mix specialty plant. She'd faced unique problems, licensing an ancient, on-premise Controls Software suite that required an expensive consultant named "Skip." Her voice on the phone sounded strained, "Mark, we're short-handed. This was the only thing Skip said we could integrate without a full rebuild." She was surviving, not transforming.

- **Chicago (Vinny DiCarlo):** And Vinny. Vinny, with his deep skepticism and pride in the old ways, simply expanded his sprawling network of shared spreadsheets. When Mark asked for an update, Vinny just sent a link to a password-protected file called "Master Production Tab 7-B" with a note: *"Mark, I got this. Trust me."*

Mark's weekly operations review had become a source of mounting anxiety. This was a Tower of Babel of digital tools. Dallas reported Cost-Per-Unit in *volume*, Phoenix in *weight*, Pittsburgh in *machine run time*. They were all claiming success, yet the consolidated corporate profit—the number that mattered—was shrinking. Mark stared at the contradictory dashboards, a cold sweat breaking out on his forehead. *I asked for a GPS, and they all bought a different language,* he thought, *and now I don't know where the hell we are.* Having it all in front of him made it painfully clear. This had become a metrics mess of huge proportions.

The crash came on the following Tuesday. Bob MacMillan, the CIO, a man who saw unauthorized cloud services as a personal insult to his network security, noticed the rogue data pipelines from Prognosys and MetricMonk. Mark hadn't bothered to get Bob's buy-in, seeing the CIO as a bureaucratic obstacle. Following protocol, Bob issued a notification which would henceforth be known to the Operations Team as "The MacAttack", and immediately shut down the connections.

The next morning, Gene Johnson's Prognosys dashboard was dark. Simultaneously, Brett Miller called Mark in a panic: "My OEE just dropped from 98% to zero! Error 404: Metric Not Found!" Mark felt a sickening wave of guilt. His digital crusade, which he thought would be his legacy, had been actively and obliviously demolished by the CIO. His failure wasn't just technical; it was a profound, strategic failure of relationship. He hadn't aligned the leadership, and now his plant managers—who had genuinely tried—were paying the price for his isolation. He felt utterly alone, holding the smoking gun of a self-inflicted debacle.

The immediate fallout from the MacAttack—Bob MacMillan's network purge—was weeks of soul-crushing political and bureaucratic recovery. Mark personally lobbied the CIO, had to secure emergency funding for VPNs, and submitted a ridiculous twenty-page security retro-application. The tools were back online, but Mark was now facing the fury of a different, equally formidable enemy: the finance department.

The week between the digital chaos and the upcoming September finance review was the most exhausting of Mark's career. He was on calls until 10 PM every night, not to fix production, but to fill out forms and mediate. He would drag himself home, too wired to sleep.

On Thursday night, he was staring blankly at his cold dinner when Emily set a glass of wine next to his plate.

"Mark, you're home but you're not *here*," she said gently, sitting across from him. "The bags under your eyes look permanent. What's wrong? I thought the digital thing was supposed to fix things, not break them."

Mark sighed, running a hand across his forehead. "It's a disaster, Em. A disaster of my own making. I bought all these fancy speedometers and fuel gauges, but I forgot that every plant is driving a different kind of vehicle. Dallas reports their cost per *volume* of product. Phoenix reports per *finished unit weight*. Pittsburgh is based on *machine run time*. They're all measuring different things differently, and the finance team—Cynthia, the Director of Financial Reporting, who is about to have a nervous breakdown—is spending a fortune manually translating all of it."

Emily, a science teacher who understood the fundamentals of logic, frowned. "So, the new digital tools... they just help them be more efficient at being *inconsistent*?"

The simplicity of her question hit him like a punch. "Exactly," Mark whispered. "I automated the existing, pre-digital nonsense. The tools were designed to make their current data easier to view, not to force them into a new, unified structure. I was so focused on shiny new software, I forgot the most basic rule of operations: **Rules before tools.** We must standardize and align on the processes and metrics before we can effectively automate them. We needed a single, shared definition of *profitability* before we could ever hope for a digital platform that could help all the plants succeed."

He spent the rest of the night reviewing the Finance team's printout, titled "Omnicron Products Plant Data Translation Schema V9.1," a grotesque flowchart that might as well have contained absurdities like: *If Pittsburgh throughput is > 5, then divide Chicago machine hours by Phoenix inventory weight. Consult Vinny if result is odd.* The sheer cost and complexity of manually translating digital data made him feel a wave of shame. He was the VP of Operations, and he had created quicksand for his dedicated teams.

The next weekend, Mark took Emily's advice and stepped away from the office entirely. He spent Saturday in the basement, trying to fix the leaking faucet on the old utility sink next to the washer. The simple manual had 12 complicated steps, requiring three different specialty tools. He realized he was trying to force a 21st-century repair on a 1970s plumbing system. He drove to the hardware store, only to find four different sizes of the seemingly simple gasket he needed, each differentiated by a millimeter he couldn't measure without the part in his hand. Of course, he bought the wrong one, necessitating a frustrated trip back. What should have taken no more than an hour turned into an entire day's adventure of trial, error, and driving. The frustration was immense, and he slammed the tool kit shut with a final thought: *Everything should just be standard so it would be easy to repair.*

"I'll fix this", Mark said to himself. "We will pick one standard for everyone and move forward from there. Everyone will measure the same way and then we can learn and share and make those improvements we need. That's it." There was an air of satisfaction and a sense that the way out of the chaos was to make definitive decisions.

CHAPTER 6: THE TRAGEDY OF DICTATION

O n Monday, determined to stop the chaos, Mark moved forward with his resolve. He issued a corporate mandate: **Prognosys**—the biggest, most expensive tool—would now be the official maintenance planning system for all four plants, following the model used by Dallas. He saw standardization as the only cure for his metrics mess.

On the surface, the initial weeks seemed promising. Each plant manager reported full installation of Prognosys, and the dashboards began flowing with pristine, unified data—at least, they appeared unified. Mark initially felt a rush of relief, believing his dictation had forced the necessary compliance. But as he began digging into the reports, a slow dread crept in. The systems were running, yes, but the data, the fundamental building blocks of his transformation, was either nonsensical, drastically inflated, or simply entered once a week in batch. What he had demanded as standardization, his plant managers had enacted as a form of subtle, bureaucratic resistance, turning his digital solution into a digital nightmare.

● ● ●

The plant managers had zero ownership in the selection of the platform, creating an immediate, passive-aggressive resistance to a system they felt was being dictated from corporate with no understanding of their floor-level realities. Forcing a tool on an unwilling or unready workforce proved to be a subtle, insidious form of sabotage. Mark began to feel a deep isolation, a growing rift with the very people he was trying to save.

At the December year end Operations Review Meeting, the plants shared their experiences.

- **Phoenix (Brett Miller):** Brett's compliance was chilling. "Mark, we've installed it! We love it!" Brett reported, but his team had spent two months and $15,000 on customization services to make Prognosys perfectly mimic the old paper forms they had used for the last 15 years. Mark looked at the new Phoenix dashboard—it was Prognosys, but it operated exactly like the old, inefficient system. *Functionally irrelevant,* he thought bitterly. Brett had won by adopting the tool without adopting the change, even in the face of the initial improvement that started the entire process.

• • •

- **Chicago (Vinny DiCarlo):** Vinny was openly defiant. He only deployed Prognosys on the two newest, easiest production lines, ignoring the high-margin, specialized legacy lines. "The legacy lines are too delicate, Mark," Vinny stated. "One wrong code in that fancy system, and we lose $200k in specialty product. We'll stick to the spreadsheet for the core business." Vinny was protecting his turf, and Mark had given him no compelling reason to risk it.

- **Pittsburgh (Rebecca Stevens):** Rebecca's slides broke Mark's spirit. "Mark," her voice was thin, "we lost our key process engineer, Alice, three months ago. We haven't replaced her. We are running 12-hour shifts just to get product out the door. We tried to support the training sessions but struggled to find the time. The on-line courses are even more time consuming and frankly are difficult to follow. So, here's our process: At 4:45 PM on the last Friday of the month, a temp manually keys the numbers into Prognosys."

Mark sat at his desk after the meeting, his head in his hands. He looked at the pristine data flowing from Pittsburgh's dashboard—data that was two days old and entered by a minimum-wage temp. He had paid $85,000 for a predictive maintenance solution and had turned it into a $5/hour data entry program.

I utterly failed to respect the capacity of my people, he realized. He hadn't just lacked a **change management plan**; he had demanded a sprinter's pace—meeting aggressive margin goals and covering for departed colleagues—while simultaneously asking them to learn a complex new system.

That night, over another quiet dinner, Emily watched him. "You're trying to move everyone forward at your speed, Mark, not theirs," she observed. "You've seen the destination, but they're still fighting to keep the lights on."

Mark looked at her, finally understanding. His failures—the Tower of Babel, the Metrics Mess, the Forced March—all stemmed from the same hubris. He was leading a **technology deployment** instead of a **human transformation.** He hadn't provided a strategy, he hadn't aligned the rules, and he hadn't respected his people's bandwidth. The digital transformation wasn't a one-time *purchase*; it was a continuous *cultivation* that required leadership, resources, and time. He had to regroup and start over. The next conference could not be about tools; it had to be about **leadership**.

The most emotionally draining day came the next day of the Plant Manager meeting. Mark knew the conflicting metrics was their biggest barrier and the biggest reason why they all couldn't just build on the initial Phoenix success.

"Look," Mark began, his voice dropping the VP of Ops tone for something more human. "I screwed up. We bought the cars before we agreed on the traffic laws. We can't move forward when Dallas says 'profitability' in kilometers and Phoenix says it in minutes."

"We are going to pause our focus on year-over-year comparisons for the time being. Those historical comparisons can sometimes unintentionally reinforce outdated practices. Moving forward, the only metric that matters is how *this year* performs against *the clear, high standard we are establishing today*. That standard will be OEE (Overall Equipment Effectiveness), measured using an absolutely consistent definition across all four plants."

The room erupted. Gene Johnson was worried about how it would reflect on his $120M plant. Rebecca Stevens in Pittsburgh was vocal. "Mark, you're asking us to rewrite 15 years of institutional knowledge! We have a complex mix—our new numbers will look terrible."

Mark met her eyes. "Rebecca, your historical numbers are a lie we've been telling ourselves. We are no longer measuring the past. We are building the future. The pain will be temporary, but the clarity will be permanent. This is not a suggestion; it is the new rule. **We fix the rules first.**" The decision was painful, but for the first time, it was clear. The new metrics—Availability, Performance, and Quality— with consistent definitions, would force them to communicate in a single, universal language.

Despite the initial resistance, the strategy, combined with the new metrics, gave the team a focus they hadn't had before. The initial adoption of the new metrics was good, driven by the plant managers realizing that finally, everyone was being measured by the same yardstick. It was a small win, a temporary truce in the transformation war, but Mark carried it like a shield back into his meetings with Brian Quince. The foundation, however painful, was finally being poured.

He brought the plant managers back at the end of January for the strategic planning meeting. His slides included the new direction.

The Mistakes: The First Try Catastrophes	The Lessons Learned
The Babel of Tools (No Strategy/Leadership): Giving out budget and freedom to buy tools without a unified strategy or securing buy-in from the CIO (Bob MacMillan) led to conflicting, unsanctioned systems and the MacAttack network shutdown.	**Executive Alignment is Non-Negotiable:** Transformation must start at the leadership level. The CIO/OT/Ops must be aligned on security, infrastructure, and the final goal before the first purchase is made.
The Metrics Mess (Rules Before Tools): The new digital tools merely automated or digitized the plant's existing, non-standard rules, forcing the finance team into expensive, manual translation of digital data.	**Align the Rules First:** The first mandate cannot be a tool purchase; it must be a corporate-wide alignment on metric definitions (e.g., OEE, Cost Per Unit). The tools must be the mechanism for reporting the new, unified reality.
The Forced March (No Change/Resources): Mark forced the most expensive tool (Prognosys) onto all plants without respecting their unique capacities. Pittsburgh lacked the **human resources** (Alice's un-replaced role) and Chicago lacked the **digital maturity**.	**Respect Human Capacity:** A change management plan is as vital as the software license. Failure to provide resources (staffing, training, time) turns expensive predictive solutions into minimum-wage data entry programs, fostering insidious resistance.

CHAPTER 7: REBUILDING WITH GRIT AND STRUCTURE

M ark spent the weeks after his digital debacle in a state of quiet, focused humiliation. He thought back to the sight of the 'Master Production Tab 7-B' link, the memory of Rebecca Stevens's defeated voice, and Emily's simple insight: *You're leading a technology deployment instead of a human transformation.* These thoughts had been enough to shatter his old conviction. He realized his failure wasn't in *what* he bought, but in *how* he led.

He decided to attend another industry conference like he had in previous years, but this time he didn't attend the splashy vendor presentations. He went to the networking lounges, seeking out the veterans, the leaders who had the scars of failure. He stopped asking, "What tool did you use?" and started asking, "How did you get the CFO to trust you?" and "What was the first conversation you had with your Plant

Managers after you screwed up?" The wisdom was simple, but profound: **Start with the people and the plan, not the product.**

Part of this new way of working was to look at how the team was organized. The successful companies, he learned, had the right people with authority working closely with the impacted departments. Mark returned and made the first, necessary structural change. He brought Thom Otter, the VP of OT, out of the CIO's orbit and had him report directly to Operations. "Thom," Mark said, leaning across the table, "You know the factory floor, I know the profit-and-loss. We need to stop building our digital house on IT's blueprint alone. I need a roadmap—not a list of tools—but a phased approach for how to unlock those 6.2 million dollars. We need a cohesive people, process, and technology roadmap to bring the plants to the same level of digital maturity and capability and then to move them forward."

Thom, a quiet, brilliant engineer, took the task personally. He spent weeks on the plant floors, mapping the true complexity of their systems. His resulting 3-year Digital Transformation Roadmap wasn't a finished book; it was a rough, directional compass. When Mark shared it with the PMs at the

April review meeting, Vinny passive-aggressively folded his arms. "Looks like more consultants' dreams," he muttered, but Mark had anticipated the resistance. This time, he didn't demand belief; he demanded engagement. The other plant managers kept their opinions to themselves, with only Rebecca offering some hope. "We shall see, and hopefully, we shall succeed" was all that she said.

● ● ●

CHAPTER 8: THE MID-YEAR CRISIS

The pressure did not abate. By the middle of this second year, the numbers were a brutal reality check. Costs were not only *not* on track, they were worse than the previous year. Mark was in Brian Quince's office almost daily, defending his new, intangible plan.

"Mark, the numbers are going in the wrong direction," Brian stated, his voice a low, dangerous register. "You promised a path to 22%, and we are sinking further from last year's 18.5%. I can't take *conviction* to the board."

Mark felt the internal tremor of fear, but he stuck to his narrative, clinging to the small wins in Phoenix and Dallas. "Brian, we've had a messy reset. We've admitted the past mistakes and are building the foundation. The Dallas Plant just had a 2% scrap reduction on one line. It's a tiny win, but it's real data, and it proves the potential. Give us until year-end to show the turn." He was gambling his career, but he knew the digital story was the only long-term path for Omnicron. He had to convince the C-suite that it was the *right* long-term path, not just the easiest.

The small wins, while personally validating for the Plant Managers, were not enough to silence the corporate anxiety. At the September financial review, the overall margin had barely budged, moving from 18.5% to a disappointing 18.8%. Mark presented the positive data points—the Dallas scrap reduction, the Phoenix availability restoration, the Pittsburgh scheduling win—with the urgency of a defense attorney fighting a losing case.

Brian cut him off before he could finish the third slide. "Mark, these are wonderful stories of operational engagement. Truly. But I am not an investor in anecdotes; I am the CFO of a company that is still short of its stated financial goals. You've saved two hundred thousand dollars in Dallas, but the $6.2 million target remains a theoretical line item. The cost of your new infrastructure and tools is still outpacing the realized savings." Brian leaned back, his expression conveying profound disappointment. "The transformation is still costing us more than it's giving us. You have until year-end to turn this from a feel-good story into a fiscal reality."

Mark left the meeting feeling the old, familiar knot of anxiety. The plants were fighting hard, and they were finally working smarter, but the complexity of a company-wide shift meant the initial expense and the sheer inertia of outdated practices were still winning the short-term war. The wins were real, but they were still localized. He had proven the *potential* of that initial win in Phoenix, but he hadn't yet proven the *scalability* across the entire enterprise.

But Thom Otter delivered that cohesive 3-year roadmap that unified the high-volume plants (Dallas, Phoenix, Pittsburgh). The finance team became the evangelists for the metric standardization. They worked with Thom and Bob MacMillan to deprecate old, redundant tools, eliminating the "crutches" to force adoption of the new digital systems. The month-end closing process, a five-day cycle of reconciliation, dropped to three days, and reporting errors decreased by 50%. This was a psychological victory, proving that process change, when supported, yields undeniable results.

But even with the new structures, one plant remained an anchor: Chicago. Vinny DiCarlo, the Plant Manager of the vital 45%-margin specialty operation, saw the new digital processes as an insult to his years of experience. Mark knew that enterprise transformation required commitment, not just compliance. The difficult decision was made to part ways with Vinny, sending a clear message to the organization: digital fluency is now a core operational competency, and the transformation is non-negotiable. His replacement was Tony Mancuso, a leader hired specifically for his deep experience with modern digital manufacturing systems and a proven track record of using software to empower, not overwhelm, floor-level operations.

CHAPTER 9: THE SHINY NEW OBJECT

A s the new year dawned, David's message was clear disappointment in the prior year's performance, but the executive team supported by Brian, was willing to give Mark a final shot to make his complex, human-centric strategy a financial success. Buoyed by the leadership change in Chicago and the infusion of a little bit of budget, the plants showed the first signs that Mark's strategy was beginning to scale. The initial small, localized victories—the $50 fix, the $300 part—were starting to compound into real, corporate-level fiscal reality. The Plant Managers, now armed with stable networks and unified metrics, moved from fixing localized errors to tackling systemic, high-value friction points.

In Dallas, Gene Johnson's team, utilizing the now-stable Prognosys system and the new real-time scrap data, targeted the long-standing issue of 'Ghost Runs'—periods when the machine was operating but producing defective product that wasn't immediately caught. By Q1, the system's predictive modeling, tuned by the new data analyst, accurately forecast a

$1.2 million reduction in specialty material waste over the coming year. This wasn't achieved by a new piece of technology, but by the plant team's ability to trust the data and adjust the chemical mix ratio *proactively*, twenty minutes before the scrap rate would historically spike. Gene presented the success to Mark, not as a tool victory, but as a "process intelligence win," finally putting a real dent in the $6.2 million target.

Phoenix followed suit. Brett and Eric focused their efforts on energy optimization, leveraging the new network stability to integrate real-time energy consumption data with the production schedule. They discovered that by simply resequencing the startup order of their heaviest machinery each morning—a change that required zero capital expenditure—they could eliminate the expensive, short-term peak demand charges that plagued their utility bills. The result was a documented $1.4 million annual saving in energy costs, validated directly by the finance team. The victory was a profound philosophical one: the most significant savings weren't hidden in complex AI, but in applying digital visibility to long-accepted, non-optimized procedures. Mark felt a surge of relief; the transformation was no longer a bluff, but a fiscally validated reality, generating nearly $3 million in annualized, verifiable savings within the first four months.

The swift turnaround in Chicago became the new internal case study. Tony, the new Plant Manager, didn't just comply with the new mandates; he actively evangelized the digital tools, seeing them as a means to empower his team. He took the standardized metrics and the newly stable systems, and instead of forcing complex corporate dashboards on the veteran floor staff, he simplified the data presentation. Tony spearheaded the development of a user-friendly, single-screen visualization for each workstation, displaying only the three key metrics the operator could directly influence: cycle time, quality defect count, and material waste. This approach successfully reframed the digital tools not as corporate surveillance, but as a real-time coach, instantly engaging his formerly skeptical operators. Within two months, this shift led to a verifiable 3% decrease in specialty material waste, proving that the right leadership, focused on human-centric digital adoption, could unlock immediate and substantial value in even the most resistant parts of the organization.

As Mark was sitting at his desk, finally starting to feel like things were coming together, there was a knock at the office door.

"Mark, you're still here. Good," CEO David McAllister said, his eyes bright. "I've just been reading about the 'Cogmagnito' AI platform. It's absolutely revolutionary. Cutting edge. I mean, *true* disruption."

Mark managed a weak smile. "I've heard of it, David. A powerful tool, supposedly."

"Powerful doesn't even cover it. It processes millions of data points simultaneously! It predicts supply chain weaknesses, optimizes energy consumption, even tells us the exact moment a piece of machinery is going to fail. We need this, Mark. We need to be a leader, not a follower." David gestured enthusiastically at the tablet screen. "I want it deployed, company-wide. I'll give you three months."

Mark swallowed. "Three months, David? With all due respect, that's... highly ambitious. We have the internal efficiency plan—the one the teams are finally gaining traction with. Integrating something this complex, with our current infrastructure, would take months of testing and custom engineering. And the licensing alone—"

"Nonsense, Mark. The article says it's plug-and-play. We have the budget. You'll find it. We can repurpose some of the funding from your current 'internal initiatives,' actually. Consider this your new top priority. I want Cogmagnito reporting operational metrics by the end of the quarter. It will pay for itself in weeks."

David's enthusiasm was a physical force, leaving no room for counterargument. Mark knew the quarter-end deadline was impossible, the cost was staggering, and diverting funds would gut their current progress. Yet, the CEO's commitment was absolute.

"Of course, David. I'll draft the deployment plan immediately. We'll push the teams to meet that timeline."

David clapped his hands together. "That's the spirit! Good work, Mark. Go home. I'll expect the first budget reallocation memo in my inbox in a few weeks."

Mark nodded, feeling the weight of the impossible task settle on his shoulders. "Good night, David."

The Cogmagnito AI platform—the CEO's shining new obsession—was a disaster that manifested almost immediately. Mark received his first wave of frantic texts from Plant Managers two days after the initial installation.

The AI, which had been promised as a plug-and-play solution, instead behaved like an uninvited, highly disruptive guest. It lacked the necessary context for Omnicron's operational friction. In Dallas, Cogmagnito identified a "catastrophic impending failure" on the Alpha-9 line and automatically halted production to initiate a full shutdown. Gene Johnson's team spent three hours troubleshooting the code before realizing the AI had simply misinterpreted a routine, 30-second pressure spike—a known common cause variation—as a sign of imminent boiler explosion. The AI, designed to prevent downtime, had instead *created* an unnecessary, costly one.

Pittsburgh's situation was worse. Because Rebecca's team still manually keyed in some production data once a month, the AI, designed to react to real-time events, found no data. It then began generating absurd, nonsensical recommendations based on its pre-loaded generic industry models. Rebecca's morning report included the AI's top suggestion: "Increase throughput by re-sequencing the high-margin Alpha-9 line to run immediately after the low-margin Zeta line." Since the Pittsburgh plant didn't even *manufacture* the Zeta line connector, the recommendation was useless. When the AI was integrated with the plant's temperature control system to "optimize energy," it instead plunged the specialty parts curing room into an unrecoverable thermal cycle, leading to the immediate scrapping of $45,000 worth of specialized product. The plant managers began treating the Cogmagnito dashboards not as tools, but as an active, hostile threat to their daily operations.

This cycle of disruption and exhaustion led Mark to figure out a way to tame the madness while still trying to move forward with the original roadmap. He realized transformation couldn't be a collaboration between three equal VPs (Process, Technology, Operations) all trying to execute different orders from the inconsistent CEO. He brought the entire Process Improvement team under his Operations umbrella and created a new, powerful role: the VP of Digital Adoption and Governance (DDAG). This VP became the face of the transformation, empowered to enforce standardized, digitally-enabled processes across all plants, aligning local preferences to the overall standards, but also nurturing the roadmap and tool deployment to ensure consistency and scalability. The message to the organization was clear: the momentum had been temporarily broken by the AI, but the new structure, anchored by unyielding grit and focused accountability, would allow them to rebuild it stronger.

This new structure proved its value almost immediately by acting as the organization's central immune system. Just weeks after the DDAG's appointment, the Dallas Plant submitted a formal request for a new, third-party application to track 'Batch Cycle Time Adherence,' claiming their current tools couldn't handle the complexity. The DDAG office reviewed the request, recognized that the Pittsburgh Plant already had set up the functionality to track the exact metric, but that the Dallas team simply hadn't been trained on the feature. The VP of DDAG denied the purchase request, not as a bureaucratic obstacle, but as a strategic enabler, committing instead to a targeted week of on-site training to unlock the existing capability, thus preserving the standardized toolset and eliminating the addition of another rogue system.

Although the new DDAG structure was showing undeniable value in standardizing metrics and preventing minor tool proliferation, its effectiveness was constantly and systematically undermined by the massive, unfocused effort required to manage the mandated AI platform. Every request the DDAG denied to maintain standardization was countered by a day spent babysitting Cogmagnito, troubleshooting its false alarms, or translating its nonsensical recommendations. The team was locked in a costly, exhausting, and losing battle, forced to dedicate their finite resources to managing the CEO's "shiny new object" rather than fueling the steady, compounding growth of the original, sound roadmap.

CHAPTER 10: THE GRINDING BATTLE FOR ADOPTION

The chaos of the mandated AI adoption quickly escalated from technical disruption to a full-blown human crisis. The constant stream of false alarms, automated shutdowns, and absurd recommendations from the Cogmagnito platform began to systematically undermine the authority and expertise of the Plant Managers and their veteran engineers. Morale plummeted as the teams, finally gaining traction with the cohesive internal roadmap, were forced to dedicate critical time to "Cogmagnito babysitting"—troubleshooting a tool that actively worked against them. Production Managers, already stretched thin, started quitting, their resignation notes citing unmanageable stress and a corporate environment that valued unproven technology over experienced judgment.

The resulting talent drain was profound. While Mark was able to hire replacements, the onboarding was agonizingly slow. Training a new engineer on Omnicron's legacy systems while simultaneously demanding proficiency in the unstable, context-less AI platform was a recipe for burnout. The institutional knowledge lost with each departure—the kind of tacit, hard-won wisdom that could never be captured in a 300-page manual—created operational voids. The company was caught in a vicious cycle: the impossible demands of the new tools and system changes caused key personnel to leave, which in turn increased the burden on the remaining staff, driving up stress, absenteeism, and ultimately, further departures. The initial hope Mark had felt was now smothered by the overwhelming reality of human exhaustion.

The axe fell in January. David McAllister, the CEO, a man who believed in the grand vision but couldn't stomach the short-term financial dip and was always enamored by the next new thing, was quietly dismissed by the board. The message was clear: The *vision* was too slow. The *cost* was too high.

Two weeks later, the new CEO was announced: Brian Quince.

Brian Quince's ascension from CFO to CEO was not a victory for Mark. It was the moment the velvet gloves came off. Brian's inaugural address was short, precise, and glacial: "We will meet the 22% margin goal. The transformation will continue, but it will be measured in dollars, not metaphors. I expect immediate, documented progress, or the funding is done."

The pressure Mark had felt from the outside was now sitting in the corner office, relentlessly focused on cost. The budget for Mark's digital initiatives was immediately slashed by 15%. Mark felt the tightening noose, but this time, he had his plant managers—his people—fighting with him. The grinding battle for adoption had begun, and it was rooted not in software, but in small, tenacious human victories.

The Turning Point: Building Momentum

Mark tasked his plant managers with finding one measurable, demonstrable win—one instance where the new tools, the aligned metrics, and the strategy had paid off in clear, undeniable dollars.

- **Dallas: Gene Johnson and the Power of Real-Time Data**

    Gene in Dallas was fighting a war on the floor.

His team, however, was starting to embrace the Prognosys system, now that the underlying network was stabilized and the metrics were unified. His breakthrough came when his shift supervisor, a skeptical man named Tom, started monitoring the new PPM (Parts Per Million) scrap dashboard.

"We had always accepted a 1.5% scrap rate on the Alpha-9 connector," Gene told Mark over a late-night call. "It was just 'normal variation.' But Tom, looking at the real-time data, noticed that the rate jumped to 4% every single time we had a raw material changeover. Before, we would just clean up the scrap and write it off. Now, the dashboard flagged the event immediately. Tom spent thirty minutes with the machine operator and realized the pre-feed sensor was misaligned only during the changeover sequence. It was a $50 fix. That single discovery is going to save us over $200,000 this year, Mark. It wasn't the software that fixed it; it was the software giving Tom the *time* and the *evidence* to be brilliant." Gene's voice was tinged with a new pride; he was finally seeing the value.

● Phoenix: Brett Miller and the Trust in the Machine

The Phoenix team, led by Brett Miller and engineer Eric Washington, was facing its own test of faith. The MetricMonk OEE tracker, now correctly configured, flagged a massive dip in Availability on one of their main lines. Brett, having been burned before, was ready to manually override the alert, convinced it was another glitch.

"The data said we were losing two hours every day, but the maintenance logs said zero," Brett explained to Mark. Eric, however, convinced him to trust the new system. They spent an entire shift standing next to the line. They finally saw it: a tiny, unmonitored air pressure valve was fluctuating slightly. It wasn't enough to trip the full fault, but it was just enough to force the *operator* to stop the machine for ten minutes every hour to manually adjust the setting. "It was human intervention masking machine failure," Brett said, shaking his head. "The operator was so good at hiding the problem, our old systems never saw it. The digital tools forced us to confront the hidden reality of the floor." The simple $300 pressure regulator replacement immediately restored the two hours of availability, adding thousands to the bottom line—and, more importantly, cementing the trust between the team and the system.

● Pittsburgh: Rebecca Stevens and the Small-Batch Scheduling Autonomy

In Pittsburgh, Rebecca Stevens, dealing with the complexity of high-mix, low-volume products, finally leveraged the scheduling autonomy Mark had granted. Their old method meant they took weeks to calculate the optimal run sequence.

"We were losing money on changeover time because we couldn't properly prioritize," Rebecca shared. "My lead scheduler, David, felt like a failure because he couldn't keep up with the complexity. He was a master of the spreadsheet, but the sheer number of variables broke the system." Using the new, streamlined metrics (Cost per Changeover), David was able to build a simple optimization model within the new planning tool. He found that by grouping specialty product runs based on a shared tooling type, rather than shared raw material, they could reduce machine setup time by a staggering 40% on their core lines. "We didn't buy a new tool," Rebecca noted, "we just gave David the time and the single, correct metric to finally optimize the chaos he was already managing. The margin on those specialty products is safe, and David looks like a hero."

Mark took those stories—the $50 fix in Dallas, the hidden two hours in Phoenix, the 40% reduction in Pittsburgh setup time—and packaged them for Brian.. He knew the battle was far from over, but for the first time, he wasn't just talking about a bluff. He was presenting small, undeniable truths delivered by his most skeptical people. The mountain was still huge, but they had found the first, solid handholds.

At the mid-year review, Mark built the following slides reflecting on the digital journey to this point.

The primary challenge at first stemmed from implementation and conflicting operational maturity across the sites.

Area	Challenge	Impact
Tool Adoption & Expectations	We pursued multiple systems that were deployed with no cohesive strategy or purpose. This initial failure led to a complete lack of plant trust and adoption and disrupted multiple departments outside of the plants.	Plants reverted to using old spreadsheets ("the crutch"), entering data late, resulting in zero real-time visibility and perpetuating a month-end data scramble.
Digital Maturity & Priorities	The Chicago specialty plant, with a highly seasoned but non-digital-savvy team, passively resisted the new tools. Furthermore, conflicting R&D requests consumed their time.	Adoption was very poor. The team continued to try to use the tools to support old, non-digital processes, undermining the new system's design.

To address the deep-seated resistance and structural flaws, we implemented critical, non-negotiable changes.

Lesson Learned / Success	Action Taken	Result & Impact
Eliminating the Crutch	We partnered with the CIO and VP of OT to systematically **deprecate all old tools** (e.g., legacy spreadsheets and systems) to force adoption of the new, standardized platforms.	Month-end reporting was mandated to be done *directly* via the new dashboards. This instantly improved the closing process from **5 days to 3 days** and **decreased errors by 50%**.
Digital Mindset & Leadership	It became clear the Chicago Plant Manager was fundamentally unwilling to adopt the required new digital processes.	The difficult, but necessary, decision was made to **replace the Chicago Plant Manager** with an external leader who possessed the necessary digital experience to drive transformation.

| Avoid Shiny Object Hunting | The new AI tools were deployed at David's mandate with an unrealistic 90-day expectation for full use and immediate value. | The plants were unable to integrate the AI, which produced bad recommendations and repeatedly "broke" their systems. Plant teams ignored the tool, leading to a major conflict meeting where the vendor blamed implementation and cited a long future roadmap. |

CHAPTER 11: THE STARS BEGIN TO ALIGN

The new CEO's mandate to slash the budget by 15% immediately translated into a grim reality for Mark and Thom Otter. The initial plan had banked on consistent investment to fund the fiber optic rollout and the full integration of the planning tools. Now, Thom's three-year roadmap was at risk of becoming a five-year crawl. Mark knew he had to face Brian Quince with an ask for budget relief, armed only with the recent, albeit small, victories.

Mark called a meeting with Brian and presented a revised financial model. "Brian, the 15% cut stalls the essential network upgrades for Pittsburgh and Chicago, the very plants that need the stability to adopt the new systems. We cannot build a high-performance system on a low-grade infrastructure. I'm asking for a staged release of the initial budget, tied to documented, quarterly improvements in key metrics. Give us Q3 funding to complete the core infrastructure, and we will deliver a 0.5% margin improvement over current levels by Q4." Mark was betting on the compounding effect of the small wins.

The argument found an unexpected ally in the new Chicago Plant Manager, Tony Mancuso. Tony, a younger leader hired for his digital fluency, had not only embraced the new tools but found a way to make them accessible to the veteran floor staff. Tony had taken the Prognosys system, which Vinny had treated as a hostile takeover, and used it to *serve* his people. Instead of forcing operators to learn a complex new screen, Tony had developed a simple, single-screen visualization for each workstation, showing only the three metrics the operator could directly impact: cycle time, quality defect count, and material waste. "The older operators were wary of the 'corporate computer'," Tony explained, "but when I showed them the screen and said, 'This is your golf score— this is how you win the day,' they were instantly engaged. They saw the digital tool not as a spy from above, but as a real-time coach. We've seen a 3% decrease in specialty material waste in two months, simply by giving them immediate, actionable feedback." Tony's early success proved that the tools were viable; the problem had always been the approach.

Mark leaned into Tony's data. "Brian, what Tony did in Chicago is the template for the entire company. The $50 fix in Dallas and the $300 fix in Phoenix are compounding. We are on the cusp of an inflection point. The money you invest now is not an expense; it's the fuel that gets us across the chasm from anecdotal wins to systemic, company-wide profitability. We can afford the cut, but it will delay the 22% goal until Year Five. Release the Q3 funding, and we hit 22% by the end of Year Four." The gamble was high, but for the first time, Mark had hard evidence and an aligned, successful leader to back his narrative.

● ● ●

CHAPTER 12: FINAL SUCCESS: THE VICTORY DINNER

D espite the remaining budget friction, a palpable sense of momentum was finally building across the organization. The localized, high-impact wins were accelerating, moving from isolated successes to a predictable pattern of improvement. Dallas, leveraging the newfound stability and real-time data, achieved a $1.2 million annualized scrap reduction in specialty materials. Phoenix documented a verifiable $1.4 million annual saving by simply optimizing their energy consumption based on digital visibility. Even the smaller Pittsburgh plant, by focusing on scheduling efficiency, had significantly improved specialty product margins. While the total corporate margin was still lagging due to the initial cost of infrastructure and the lingering effects of the AI debacle, the individual plant performance was undeniable. Once Cogmagnito was decommissioned, the team regained momentum on the original roadmap. Morale was visibly growing as the teams, trusting the new metrics and systems, moved from *troubleshooting* to *optimization*. The numbers were beginning to reflect not just tool adoption, but the successful shift to a new digital mindset where data was no longer a burden, but a guide to profitability.

By the end of Year Four, the transformation was complete. The company, Omnicron Products, Inc., was no longer fighting for scraps; it was thriving. The $310 million in revenue was now generating a stunning 24% margin. Total profit had leaped to over $74.4 million. But the most important metric, the one Mark Donaldson felt in his bones, was the mood. Work was *fun* again.

The victory was celebrated on a cold January night in Chicago, high above the glittering cityscape, at the famed Everest restaurant. It was a dinner not for the C-suite, but for the people who made the change real: the Plant Managers.

Earlier in the day, Mark had presented the summary of the entire journey that led them to this success.

Lesson Learned	Narrative Summary of Failure/Insight	Recommended Action
1. Rules before Tools	Finance was forced to manually reconcile disparate plant metrics because digital tools automated existing, non-standard nonsense.	Standardize processes and metrics *before* implementing digital automation tools.
2. Priority Conflicts	Chicago plant resisted deployment because the team was overwhelmed by conflicting R&D and core business priorities.	Clearly communicate and align digital transformation priorities with core business objectives to avoid resource and focus conflicts.
3. Human and Digital Infrastructure	Pittsburgh failed to deploy the new tool because they had lost a key engineer; The $7 million "Copper-to-Fiber" overhaul and the approval of dedicated data analyst positions.	Ensure both robust foundational digital infrastructure and dedicated, skilled personnel are in place before and during deployment.

4. Cultural shift to digital mindset	The Chicago Plant Manager, Vinny DiCarlo, had to be replaced because he was fundamentally unable to adopt the new digital processes.	Address cultural resistance and replace leadership who cannot or will not adopt the necessary digital processes and mindset.
5. Eliminate the crutch	VP of Ops deprecated old tools to force adoption of the new dashboard, leading to a 50% reduction in month-end errors.	Mandate the adoption of new tools by officially retiring or deprecating the older, inefficient systems.
6. Change Management Plan	The "Forced March" to standardize on Prognosys led to passive-aggressive resistance and functionally irrelevant "compliant" deployments.	Implement a well-paced, collaborative change management plan instead of a forced, top-down deployment.

7. Deploy with the right expectations	Internal IT deployed a buggy in-house system and the CEO forced an AI tool adoption with an unrealistic 90-day expectation.	Ensure stable systems are deployed and set realistic timelines for adoption, especially for cutting-edge technology like AI.
8. Know the digital maturity	The highly seasoned Chicago team was not digitally savvy and continued to try and use new tools with old processes.	Assess the team's digital readiness and provide necessary training to ensure new tools are used to their full potential, not with old mental models.
9. Have an overall strategy with multiple phases (Have a vision)	Plants picking different, expensive tools without a unified strategy led to the "Babel of Digital Tools."	Establish a clear, unified, phased digital strategy to guide tool selection and prevent fragmentation.

• • •

10. Senior leadership support (Executive alignment)	CIO Bob MacMillan unwittingly sabotaged the initial effort by cutting off access due to a lack of alignment; The CIO later became an evangelist and convinced the C-suite to support the long-term vision.	Secure and maintain clear, consistent executive alignment and support throughout the transformation effort.
11. Avoid shiny Object Hunting	CEO learned of new AI tools and demanded their immediate adoption with high expense and no clear roadmap.	Base technology adoption on strategic need and clear roadmaps, not on impulse or the latest trends.
12. Avoid low ball budget	Tools became slow, crashing, and untrusted because IT lacked the necessary budget to maintain and stabilize the systems.	Allocate a sufficient, realistic budget for the ongoing maintenance, stability, and future development of digital systems.

13. Have a realistic timeline	Low budget and unrealistic timelines led to high tension and low trust; New CEO's first action was to grant appropriate budget and time for infrastructure fixes and personnel.	Establish realistic timelines and budgets, and be willing to adjust them to build trust and ensure success.

"I remember sitting in my office two years ago, thinking we were done for," Gene Johnson, the Dallas Plant Manager, admitted, lifting his glass of Bordeaux. His face, once lined with the worry of running the largest plant on the worst network, was relaxed. **"That copper wiring was an anchor on my soul. Every time I tried to pull a five-minute historical trend to troubleshoot a line, the entire plant network would freeze. We were literally troubleshooting a $120 million facility with a network that couldn't handle Netflix. Every minute of idle time felt like a personal failure, like I was letting my crew down."** He paused, looking directly at Mark. "Now? Operation Copper-to-Fiber is complete. My dashboard loads in two seconds. I can show my operator the cost of an idle minute *in real-time*. We're a team, not just a collection of exhausted individuals fighting blind."

● ● ●

Brett Miller, the Plant Manager from Phoenix, chimed in, leaning forward with the intensity of a convert. **"For us, the biggest difference was realizing we couldn't just have data, we needed *prospectors* to dig out the gold. Eric, my engineering manager, was spending 80% of his day manually compiling reports. He was a genius, and we had turned him into a glorified data-entry clerk."** Brett raised his glass toward the C-suite table. "The data analyst position, Sarah—that was the real game-changer. Eric and Sarah working together, dedicated purely to optimization, found the pattern in the curing temperature fluctuations. They reduced our scrap rate by 8%. That's $2 million straight to the bottom line, Mark. Before, we were throwing money away, and we didn't even know it, because we were too busy running reports to find the *why*."

Rebecca Stevens from Pittsburgh, who managed the complex, high-mix specialty plant, was beaming as she talked to Brian. "My plant is the smallest, the one with the most item codes, and we were constantly losing process engineers because the work was so frustratingly manual," she explained. **"We were the ones entering the numbers at 4:45 PM on Friday—turning that expensive software into a time clock. But with the scheduling autonomy and**

the new real-time metrics? We now sequence our high-margin runs based on actual capacity, not a quarterly forecast. We're the most efficient plant per square foot, and we know it. We stopped surviving the day and started *designing* the week."

Finally, Tony Mancuso, the new Chicago Plant Manager, stood to toast. **"In this plant, the spreadsheets were the fortress, and the old leadership was right to protect them when corporate was giving us shiny toys with no plan. But when we rolled out the new visualizations with the standardized metrics, the team finally saw the truth in the data."** Tony took a dramatic sip of his wine. "The data proved my gut right: the corporate scheduler was costing us 15 points of margin by sandwiching our specialty runs. The transformation wasn't a magic wand; it was having the right information to fight the right battles, and the leadership to back us up."

Mark stood up, tapping his spoon against his glass. All eyes turned to him—his leadership team, his plant managers, and the C-suite that had finally believed in them.

"When this journey began, we were trying to digitally transform the company," Mark began, his voice thick with emotion. "But the real transformation wasn't in the fiber optic cable or the new software dashboard. The real transformation was in us. We learned that digital transformation isn't about technology; it's about giving incredible people the tools and the time they need to be brilliant."

He raised his glass high. "To Omnicron Products, Inc. We were given a monumental task, and we faced every failure, every infrastructure block, and every budgetary doubt. We didn't just meet the challenge; we conquered it. To the 24% margin, to profitability, and to working at a company where coming to work is *fun* again."

The glasses clinked, a resounding, joyous sound that echoed the ultimate victory: they had beaten the odds, not just with software, but with solidarity. They didn't just save the company; they rebuilt it, stronger and smarter than ever before.

Mark finally got home, the warmth of the house a welcome contrast to the late January chill outside. He was tired, but the exhaustion was a pleasant one—the feeling of a long, difficult job completed with success. He slept soundly for the first time in years.

When Mark woke up Saturday morning, the world outside was silent, muted by a fresh, heavy layer of snow. He stood at the window, looking down at his driveway, contemplating the six inches of white powder awaiting his shovel. It was an intimidating task: manual, repetitive, and requiring sheer physical effort. He sighed, picturing the long, strenuous morning ahead.

Emily, already dressed, walked up behind him, setting a mug of coffee on the sill. "Thinking about the tyranny of the shovel?" she asked, her voice light. Mark chuckled. "I am. It's inefficient, archaic, and requires significant CapEx in Advil afterward. If only I could apply a little digital transformation here." Emily smiled, taking a slow sip of her coffee. "Who says you can't? Go check the garage, Mark. I took your journey to heart while you were rebuilding the company."

ABOUT THE AUTHOR

Geoffrey C. Jackson

Geoffrey Jackson has over 35 years of industrial experience beginning as a process engineer, working up to plant manager, and on to corporate Engineering and OT management roles within Operations. He has worked in multiple industries including aerospace and building materials and has extensive  knowledge of Lean and Six Sigma tools, specifically how these work in the Industry 4.0 space. He has led the digital transformation effort from concept to operationalization for a large, multi-facility company and transformed the operations of a global software provider. He is the founder and CEO of Jackson Consulting Group, LLC.

https://jcg-llc.com

www.ingramcontent.com/pod-product-compliance
Lightning Source LLC
Chambersburg PA
CBHW070434290526
45791CB00005B/1972